How To Analyze People

~

The Subtle Art of Reading and Interpreting Other People

By
Jules Dean

Table of Contents

Introduction	1
Chapter One: Why You Should Analyze People	3
Chapter Two: Body Language	5
Chapter Three: Conversation	15
Chapter Four: Spotting Someone's Mood	17
Chapter Five: Deception	24
Chapter Six: Master Your Body Language	28
Final Words	35

© Copyright 2017 by Jules Dean - All rights reserved.

It is not legal to reproduce, duplicate, or transmit any part of this document in either electronic means or in printed format. Recording of this publication is strictly prohibited.

ISBN-13: 978-1545248867
ISBN-10: 1545248869

Introduction

Congratulations on downloading this book! You're on your way to reading the people around you in completely new ways.

By now you've probably realized that so much communication is unspoken. We live in a world of insinuation, interpretation and connotation. Much is left unsaid in every single interaction we have with our friends, our family, and our coworkers.

In order to become successful, whatever your definition of success may be, we need to learn to pick up on the many subtle signals that are passed between people. This book will help you begin to interpret those unspoken signals with ease. You'll be able to read between the lines like never before!

Simply being able to "read" your friends, your family, or your coworkers will help you understand what their words aren't saying. You can be more compassionate, without forcing your partner to voice every little detail. You can be more intuitive, and deliver more in the relationships in your life because you understand more about the people you care about. You can quickly defuse your boss before he or she gets too wound up. You can learn to spot a lie!

In this book, you will read about the science behind these common interactions. You will learn to pay attention to the details of people around you, in order to deduce their inner intentions or feelings.

Don't wait another day to start paying attention! Don't wait another second to read the people in your life. Don't let your job or your relationships suffer any longer because you only know how to understand people on the surface. Dive deeper today by reading this book!

Chapter One: Why You Should Analyze People

How would you feel if someone told you a story with the caveat that "you're only going to hear about 7% of the truth?"

Would you believe that story? Would you make decisions based on the information you received in that story? Would you trust your life to that 7%?

Researchers at UCLA attempted to break down the total amount of information that gets passed between two people who are having an in-person conversation. Only that precious 7% of information comes directly and immediately from the literal words passed between people. Over half, (55% or more) comes from body language, which is how you stand, how you position your arms, how your head tilts and what your face is doing while you speak. The remaining 38% is from your vocal inflection, your tone, and the way you deliver your words.

Now consider reading a transcript of a conversation. You read only the words passed between people. Remember that you're only getting 7% of the full picture. Those people could be gesturing to each other wildly, casting sarcastic tones. You might read a conversation and misinterpret what the other person is actually saying.

That's why the art of "reading" people has become so important. This is like learning to speak all over again, with the knowledge that the unspoken human language is much more important than the literal words that are exchanged. You are embarking on a journey of observation and perception. You are deciding to immerse yourself in the deeper elements of conversation that run our lives.

By learning this language, you will be able to unlock the other side of your life, the unspoken life. You'll understand the inflections and gestures people make, even when they are unknowingly giving you more information than they intended. You will learn about body language, speech patterns, deception, and more. Then you will learn to watch for these things, both in other people and yourself! Control the massive amount of information that you yourself emit into the world without speaking. Comport yourself accordingly in any situation without betraying how you really feel!

The large majority of information communicated between two people is unspoken. Isn't it about time you learned the unspoken language?

Chapter Two: Body Language

In this chapter you will learn the other major component of language, that which comes from our body posture. You will learn to pay attention to the way people "set up" during a conversation, and be able to read them based on the many signals their bodies give off, most often completely without them knowing it!

Space and Presence

First and foremost, recognize that in any conversation, or meeting, we as participants take up space. (That's not all we do, but the space we take up is important.) Our evolution has taught us to acknowledge and pay special attention to the people who take up lots of room. We focus on the big objects. This doesn't mean overweight people, so much as it means that we pay attention to people who "command a presence" in a room. People who stand appear to take up more room, they appear larger. When people have large, sweeping gestures with their arms, they take up still more space. This is a method for commanding a room: occupy a defined space within that room.

People who sit compactly in the corner appear to be "less," and therefore can command less of a presence in the room. When you are seated, as often happens in corporate settings, sit up straight. Open your shoulders. This is a way to maximize your presence in the room. Slouching and crouching are ways to minimize the space you take up.

By "commanding" more space, you can increase the perceived power of your position to the other people in the room.

Position of the Body

The way we orient ourselves is the next major component of body language. It isn't just about being "big" in a room. If that were all there was to it, every meeting would be full of people doing jumping jacks!

The first key to posture is to thinking about it as equating to confidence and equality. Being a confident participant in a conversation has a completely different physical profile than being uncertain and fearful.

Confident individuals square up their bodies to face the person talking. This is a way of projecting yourself to the other person or people. It appears to emanate strength and confidence. People who are unsure of themselves will turn away, and appear to "deflect" potential conflict away from them.

It can also be perceived as disrespectful to face away from someone. It appears dismissive and subtly rude, because you are not providing your full (postured) attention to the conversation or the speaker. In order to be respectful, to project confidence and equality, be sure to stand or sit up straight, and face the conversation or the speaker!

These are simple signals that can help you read a room silently. The next time you're in a meeting, scan the room's participants with your eyes. Measure how much each person is "squaring up." This is a quick way to gauge confidence and aspiration. An aspiring person will want to appear confident, calm and powerful, and may unknowingly broadcast these same signals in order to command the appearance they are searching for. Keep reading to learn whether or not they're faking it!

Crossed Arms or Legs

Read that same room and pay attention to the arms and legs of the people present. In almost any situation, crossed arms or legs can be distinct defensive or "closed" signals. Imagine a young child who has not gotten what they want, despite asking or throwing a tantrum. They are standing or sitting on the floor, arms crossed, face scrunched, pouting!

The roots of this posture are familiar to most people. By attempting to appear calm and relaxed, a person with crossed arms is actually broadcasting that they are not open to the conversation in progress. You're most likely to see this posture when a contentious point is being made by someone. Half of the room may agree, and the half that disagrees will start to display closed posture.

The next time you're about to ask for a raise, or if you're trying to convince someone of a new piece of information, pay close attention to how "open" they are in that moment. By detecting these closed signals, you might decide to save your idea or your request for later. After all, this may simply mean the person isn't ready in that moment to hear you. We close off when we are in bad moods, if we're upset for any reason we can become unsusceptible to new information.

Appearing Relaxed (Casual Posture)

Yet another way to communicate one's power is to show a room or a participant how comfortable they are in their role. At first glance, you might walk into your boss's office to find him or her reclined in their chair, arms behind their head (maybe their feet are even up on their desk!) This is no mistake. They are not being lazy (unless you've caught them sleeping).

You should recognize first of all that they have spread out, and made themselves and their presence larger. This evokes the same effect as someone standing tall and gesturing widely. Our instinct is to recognize the power of this position. But this posture has a second, complementary effect. By appearing relaxed, the person also projects a different kind of confidence. Without being stern, or overbearing, the person is showing you that they feel comfortable enough in their power or their knowledge to "settle in."

Reading the Eyes and the Face

You've probably heard that "the eyes tell a story." Or that "the eyes are the window to the soul." The truth is that our eyes are very communicative, and by paying attention to the eyes of other people you can read into what they're saying. For many years, we as a society have paid attention to the eyes in order to understand other people. For this reason, some of the behaviors to watch for with the eyes are behaviors of deception, since people are knowingly trying to make their eyes evoke a certain message with you. We'll discuss that more in "deception."

Pay attention to the amount someone blinks. A normal blink rate is somewhere between 6 to 10 per minute, or about 1-2 times every ten seconds. Blinking more than that can betray another emotion is happening beneath the surface, most often attraction. If you find someone blinking more than 2-3 times per ten seconds, then they may be attracted to you!

The direction of someone's gaze is meaningful. One study actually paid attention to the eye contact and direction of contestants of the game show Jeopardy. When these contestants were being asked to recall stored old information from their memory, they almost always looked to the left! This is a reflex that most people have, when trying to recall information, we look to the left! Some theories suggest that side of the brain is important here.

Our left brains are rational and more scientific, so when we are trying to access memorized information, we look left. When we look right, we are being more creative. Creative thinking shows up in several situations. When we are bored, our minds wander, we imagine scenarios, and technically we are being creative! Pay attention to the direction people's gaze takes when not making eye contact.

Pupillary size is relevant. Your pupils are the black centers of your eyes, which change size to accommodate how much light is available in your environment. They grow to let in more light, so you can focus in lower light conditions. They constrict when light is readily available. That's why a doctor shines a light in front of your eyes during a checkup, to monitor this movement. That change happens without you realizing it, or controlling it. Your pupils move without conscious effort or control, but they also respond to your emotions and interest. Your pupils dilate, or expand, when you are interested in something. Whether it's a topic of interest, or a person of interest, your pupils will grow.

When someone makes eye contact with you, they are interested. However, people can be interested either positively or negatively. Don't count on eye contact to always be the former! No matter what, the attention of someone else is known to elicit an "arousal" response from us. If we're being stared at, it can make us uncomfortably heightened with our awareness. If we're being stared at by someone we *want* to stare at us, the arousal response is still an increased awareness, but it's positive.

Have you ever heard the phrase "I feel like I'm being watched?" The feeling is familiar to many people, because the attention of other people elicits a palpable response. Eye contact and attention is one of the most obvious signals that will signal someone's keen focus on you, because you'll feel it instinctively!

The duration of eye contact is something to watch for. It may vary from culture to culture, but in general a sustained eye contact is considered respectful during a conversation. Stare too long, and eye contact can become uncomfortable. In this way, sustained eye contact can be used to intimidate other people.

What if someone purposefully isn't making eye contact with you? This can signal fear, not necessarily a liar. We make eye contact when we are interested, engaged, and confident in some way. A skittish glance can signal simply the opposite: someone who is worried, or fearful of your response.

Now consider the eyebrows. We use our eyebrows primarily to express some kind of discomfort. Most people are familiar with the shocked expression that raises both eyebrows. Think about that scene in Home Alone where he looks in the mirror and screams!

Surprise or shock are forms of discomfort for the human face. Well, keep that in mind when reading someone's eyes. If they have raised eyebrows during a conversation, and they aren't being actively scared by some kind of scary movie, then they are experiencing discomfort with the conversation. Something being said is affecting them negatively, and causing them some amount of doubt, uncertainty, or fear.

The human face and head are actually very good at betraying our anxiety. When you're talking to someone, and they're nodding frequently or significantly, this is often another way we express anxiousness. Try to remember the last difficult conversation you had with someone. While you were talking, were they solemnly nodding their head as they listened? This is a good indication that what you're saying is landing deeply with them, possibly causing them that discomfort. Maybe they felt that discomfort for you, as an empathetic response! The head nod is a way to tell.

Anxiousness is different than stress. Stress is something we often feel about ourselves and our own lives. When a person is feeling stress, you'll be able to tell from the jawline. Clenched jaws are fast ways to divine that someone is starting to feel stress. A clenched jaw just projects tension, doesn't it?

Reading the Smile

Our smiles are natural indicators of happiness. They flow out of us, they erupt in laughter, and they can signal so many other things.

One of the most consistent things to look for when trying to understand the truth behind a smile are actually the eyes! A "duchenne" smile is a true smile. When we smile truthfully, the wrinkles at the corners of our eyes become visible. We "smile with our eyes" when we mean it.

This is one of the best examples of looking for "clustered" signals. As people; we use our faces, bodies, words, and voices all simultaneously to communicate, we can only control so much at once. The rest we leave to our instincts. We may therefore smile in an effort to convince someone of our happiness, but we cannot often control the other elements of the smile beyond our mouths! Look to the eyes to judge a real smile from a fake one. We'll review these clusters in the "deception" section.

Gesturing

The way we move our hands and our arms can communicate the truth behind our words. A gesture can betray an emotion, an aspiration, a belief or a feeling. Here are a few of the major gestures to start looking for, along with what they are most likely to mean.

The shoulder shrug. The shoulder shrug is one of the globally understood gestures that means "... I don't know!" It involves several components. A simple shrug may just be a small shoulder raise toward the ears. This actually carries meaning, because this gesture is a subconscious method of protecting the neck. In this way, it's actually what's known as a submissive gesture, like a dog might use when submitting to the will of a more powerful dog. By admitting we don't know something, we are opening ourselves to the will of someone else, who might know. It is a way of showing vulnerability so that a connection can be made. The other components of the shrug support this effort. Open palms during a shrug make it even more elaborate, because they are also indicative of submission. We are showing the other person we have nothing to hide, and we are not a threat because of this.

Finally, a shrug can have lifted eyebrows, a sign of discomfort with not knowing. By showing this submissive posture and gesture, we are actually inviting the participation and involvement of the other person. In this way, shrugs can act as a greeting!

Open palms

We mentioned the use of open palms during a shrug to show submission, because the open palms show the other person we have nothing to hide. For the same reason, open palms by themselves are a display of honesty. Consider the many ways we use open palms in our gestured communication.

A big hug can start with open arms, and open palms. This is a signal of honest openness, nothing to hide, and a simple wish for affection. What about the use of open palms above the head? "I surrender!" A surrender must be honest if it is to succeed, so you display how you aren't hiding anything by holding your open palms above your head.

The finger point. This is an intimidation gesture, in which the person closes their hand except for their index finger. This finger is held out in front of the person toward their "victim." Some researchers contend that this is so intimidating because the index finger actually imitates a weapon that the person is holding toward you.

Fidgeting legs. We can sometimes keep our emotions in check, but one of the ways our anxiousness can escape is from the bottom up! If you see a tapping foot, or a fidgeting leg, this is a good indicator of anxiousness.

In this chapter you've learned the basics for observing someone else's body language. Remember that body language accounts for over half of all communication between people. In the next chapter, you'll learn about the nonverbal side of vocal communication!

Chapter Three: Conversation

In this chapter you will learn to listen past the words people are saying, and understand how the way they are saying the words can change everything.

Analyzing conversation is an art. Everyone is different, and has different mannerisms that affect their delivery of vocal communication. But these guidelines will help you understand a little bit better what is happening.

Vocal Quality

The perceived consistency or "strength" of someone's voice is an indication of confidence and relaxation. A smooth, deliberate vocal quality can reveal that someone is comfortable and deliberate in what they are saying to you.

Vocal Volume

Volume is an indicator of certainty in the same ways as vocal quality. If someone's volume is constant, and comfortable, you can believe what they are saying. They are delivering their words in a relaxed way. It's variability in volume that you need to pay attention to. Very soft words can indicate worry or fear, as well as shame. Louder volumes can indicate deceit.

Vocal Tone

Depending on if you are observing a man or a woman, then vocal tone is important to pay attention to. When men are attracted to someone, they drop their voice into their deeper tones, usually without even knowing it. Women, on the other hand, are more likely to raise their vocal tone to higher registers when attracted or interested in someone. Pay attention to someone's "normal" vocal tone, and then listen for major deviations when they talk to different people!

Vocal Speed

The speed of our voice can betray worry or anxiousness. When someone's conversation becomes hurried or sped up in any way, they are often nervous!

In this quick chapter you have learnt the basics of observing someone's vocal tone and quality in order to understand how confident someone is who is talking to you! The tone and quality and other characteristics of the voice are almost four times more informative than the actual words the person is saying, so pay close attention! For extra practice, be sure to pay attention to the way people talk to each other, rather than just you. Our posture, our voice and our attention change drastically from one person to the next!

Chapter Four: Spotting Someone's Mood

In this chapter you will learn how to identify the major moods that can be visible or detectable through body language and vocal variety. Learning to spot someone's mood can be a critical component of any interaction. This is the foundation to reading a room. It's not enough to read individual signals from someone, you need an insight that you can act on. Moods and intentions are what we can do something about. We can change our approach to a conversation with our boss if they're mad or unreceptive. We can soften our words when we realize a loved one is in pain. These are the things that make us more understanding, helpful individuals.

Identifying Anger

Anger can appear in different ways. Some people are explosive when they're angry. They become loud, and intimidating. These people are easy to identify when they're angry. It's the quiet anger that can be difficult, because it remains in the background until you've hurt their feelings even further. First and foremost, look for this quiet anger when someone is in "closed" or "defensive" postures. Closed arms show you that the person is in one of these postures. When we become angry, we don't want to let people in, accept new ideas or even relax. This is the second series of gestures or postures to look for: stressful tension. Anger creates tension, so look for the clenched jaw. Look for tense shoulders. Look for agitation in the legs. These are the keys to uncovering subtle anger!

Identifying Frustration

Frustration is another form of tension when it's being expressed through human posturing. Someone who is frustrated will reduce their presence in a room. They'll posture as someone who is defeated. Someone who is defeated will slouch, close off, sit rather than stand, or otherwise become more compact. On top of that, they will display discomfort or disagreement when someone is talking about the frustrating subject. The eyebrows will rise as a sign of discomfort. Arms and/or legs will close off, and they will face slightly away from the person talking. Look also for a furrowed brow to indicate frustration or displeasure.

Identifying Fear or Nervousness

Some research suggests that fear is a completely different bodily state. Our sweat becomes different, our mood and posture all change drastically. Someone who is scared will physically distance themselves from what they are scared of, so pay attention to where the person is set in the room.

A few extra feet can be the difference. It also matters where they "point" themselves. If a person is facing you directly, they are engaged and attentive. But check their feet. If the feet are pointed away from you, it may be a signal of unhappiness or even fear.

We subconsciously point our feet toward what we want or where we want to be. Look for someone pointing themselves toward the exit if they're uncomfortable and want to leave. When we are fearful, our body posture and positioning can revert to our evolutionary instinct. If someone's hands rise up to cover the neck, it can signal fear or anxiousness.

Identifying Boredom

Boredom should be easy to spot, when you know what you're looking for. People who have become bored will generally look at anything in the room, except the normal focal point (the person talking). Any kind of repeated action is a boredom signal, because we are trying to give our focus something to do. Look for a foot tapping, a pencil being played with, etc.

Boredom is not always bad for you. A bored person may be perfectly ready to take the next step in the process being discussed. If you're selling something or someone on a new concept, and you start to detect boredom, it may very well be because you've done a good job thus far and they are simply ready to follow you on to the next step. Identify this as quickly as you can so you can keep things moving. Boredom can be a killer for emotional bond!

Closed Off, Unreceptive

We have many signals to use when we are feeling closed off, or unreceptive to new ideas. Our mood dampens in this state, so our posture gets worse, we slouch, and we constrict. Look for the telltale crossing of arms or legs when you're talking to someone, this will be a clear signal that they aren't being receptive to what you're delivering. If you're negotiating something, these signals will tell you the person isn't responding to your current line of reasoning. It's probably best to hit the brakes, and try a new angle. Focus on opening them up further before pitching again.

Open or Receptive

Someone who is open to suggestion will exhibit open qualities by leaving arms uncrossed, facing you directly, and maintaining comfortable eye contact. Their feet will be facing toward you, not away toward the exit. They will listen intently, look for even minor pupil dilation to indicate interest and engagement.

Interpreting Touch

Touch can be tricky. The appropriate time and placement vary from culture to culture, but touch is most often a common greeting and goodbye.

For men, touch is very sensitive in a professional environment. Consider a quick pat on the back, from one man to another. A pat in the center of the back can convey friendship and support, while a pat higher up the back toward the nape of the neck can signal dominance. An older man may firmly grip a younger man's neck in a way that actually conveys this kind of hierarchy (think father and son).

Touch is a delicate balance, always. Pay attention to the body language associated with the touch more than the actual act itself. This will teach you want you need about the power dynamics involved!

Engaged or Attracted

One signal we haven't discussed much yet is humor. It's one of the strongest ways to identify whether someone is strongly engaged, even attracted to you. If they laugh with you, if they respond to your humor, then they are aligning themselves with you for a more personal relationship.

Someone who is interested will square their bodies toward you, and participate in a process called "mirroring." Mirroring is when another person copies your body language during a conversation.

Mirroring is a subconscious way of aligning ourselves with someone else. Here's a tip: the next time you're in a meeting with someone in a position of higher power relative to everyone else in the room, make a quick note of how that person establishes themselves. Are they sitting, legs crossed? Is their hand up by their chin? Are they reclining? Now, over the course of the rest of the meeting, watch for mirroring.

Look for other members of the meeting to slowly, subconsciously, adopt that person's stance or posture. They are trying to align themselves with the person in power, or the person they are interested in. If you're that person, run a little experiment! Adopt a posture, and wait for others to mirror you. Once you see it in progress, switch it up! Uncross your legs, or lean back. Wait for the others around the table to mirror you, and sure enough, they'll start doing it!

Remember the vocal variety that is present in subtle communication? If someone is attracted to you, their voice will change. Women's voices will drift into the higher registers, while men's voices will drop an octave. They won't realize they're doing it! But you will.

Attraction or engagement will both result in pupil dilation, and increased rates of blinking. To remember this, recall the cartoons of a beautiful woman batting her eyelashes at a handsome man! That's founded on real body language, in which an increased rate of blinking silently signals to the partner an attraction.

In this chapter you have learned how to identify certain patterns of body posture to ascertain someone's mood. Pay attention to overall posture, to eyes and speech patterns to learn the underlying feelings of another person. Watch a room full of people, and use their body postures to learn the true power dynamics that are at play. Identify whether someone is open or closed to new ideas, whether they are engaged or fearful, and use this information to your advantage!

Chapter Five: Deception

So far we have discussed the major signals for moods like fear and attraction. We have learned about eye movement, facial expressions and body posturing. But these are not perfect secrets! Many people understand some elements of body posture and facial expression, enough to try to manipulate them during times of duress. That's why some of the things you would expect to indicate a lie, actually do not! Because people are more likely to consciously manipulate one or two items, you will need to understand the bigger picture of deceptive body language in order to spot a lie.

This method of assessing someone's overall body posture and unspoken communication is called "clustering," because it takes into account multiple signals, without looking simply for a single "tell" to identify a mood or deception. Clustering is the most reliable method for understanding someone else, because it takes into account many data points.

Spotting a Lie: Eyes

We are accustomed to thinking of a liar has having "shifty eyes." In funny movies, a deceitful character will have (maybe a pencil thin mustache) a shifty glance when no one is looking. That's what we expect when we are being told a lie- we expect someone to break eye contact and shy away from us. The sheepish lie is a common understanding, which is why it is more easily manipulated by people who want their lie to be believed. For this reason, it's actually sustained, intense eye contact that is a better judge of a potential lie. Ask yourself, "is this eye contact really necessary or comfortable?" If you find yourself wondering about the duration of eye contact, it probably means the person is holding it too intensely.

Sustained eye contact with fewer blinks is usually a conscious effort on the part of the liar to convince you of the truth. In this case, the words being used matter as well. Pay attention to unnecessary details, and larger words. When someone strays from their standard vocal variety and storytelling mannerisms, especially when coupled with intense eye contact, a deliberate lie is probably being woven for you!

The other component of eye language to watch for is the direction of the gaze, when not focused on you. Remember that we have an instinct to look right and left depending on the content of our thoughts. A look to the left (their left) is an effort to recall discrete information from the memory. A look to the left is like performing a search in a database. But a look to the right, however, is more common when "creative" thinking is underway. The person is creating something new, painting a picture with their mind! That's why a casual look to the right while talking is more indicative of potential dishonesty than the left. When in doubt, remember that Jeopardy contestants look left!

The Telltale Four

The next pieces to detecting potential deception are another cluster. These four signs can indicate to you that the person talking is being untruthful, and they should look somewhat familiar.

- They touch their hands
- The lean away from you
- They touch their face
- They cross their arms

You might be wondering about some of these, because they can also be used to indicate things like fear or anxiousness. That's what lying does to us! It makes us scared of being found out, which creates a significant state of anxiousness.

When someone touches their face, they are adopting a slightly defensive posture of protection from you. The touching of hands indicates nervousness as well. By leaning away, the person is increasing a protective distance from you, out of fear (of being caught) and anxiety. Crossing of the arms doesn't just meant they are resisting negotiation, it is defensive and closes them off from you. Someone who is lying wants to close off and remove further opportunity to be found out in their deception. They want to deliver the lie and end the interaction. To this end, the body responds by increasing tension and closing off, to protect them!

In this chapter you have learnt how to read a person for the various context clues of a potential lie! Remember that just one of these clues does not make someone a liar. That's why you need to read people for the many clues that together can form the picture of someone who is crafting a story and trying to convince you it's real. Look for the anxiousness and fear of someone who is closing themselves off to you, overcompensating with their eye contact, or angling themselves to escape a conversation. Watch their eye direction, and look for the creative mind at work!

Chapter Six: Master Your Body Language

In this chapter you will review the major components of body language, this time with yourself in mind! The world is full of these silent signals, and reading them can be your key to success in any of your many relationships, both personal and professional. The other side of that equation is to make sure you use your own body language effectively!

Start with your Posture

This is the easiest thing to control, especially since it's often the first impression people are going to have of you. The moment you walk into a room, your posture and your presence will be felt (or not) by the rest of the people there. In order to emanate confidence, and command respect, it's important to carry yourself in a powerful posture. Keep a straight, upright back, and open your shoulders. This spread is the way to command a wider presence that will automatically grant you a level of respect and recognition. Be careful as you sit not to slouch into the chair. Remain erect, maintain your shoulder posture.

Face Others

When you're part of a conversation, casually make sure you are addressing the participants. Keep note of where your feet are, and point them toward the conversation. You don't have to constantly re-address each new person talking, unless they speak at length. Simple by squaring up to the speaker, you are showing them that you are interested, intrigued, and confident enough to display that.

As a speaker, they will subconsciously appreciate this level of attention. They will be grateful to you for delivering it and you will stand out even as an audience member. Then, when it's your turn to speak, maintain your wide profile and watch as the other members of the audience pay you their attention.

Smile Often, Smile Genuinely

It might seem silly at first, but controlling this part of your body language can actually pay major dividends for you, too.

Not only are people drawn more to those who smile often, but smiling has actually been shown to change the chemical balance of your hormones. If you constantly tell your body that something is difficult by frowning or grimacing, like a task at work, you body actually responds by releasing stress hormones. Smiling prevents these hormones from wreaking havoc on your ability to accomplish challenging things!

Be Engaging, Be Open

We all want things from our relationships. When we are at work, we want our colleague's respect and admiration. We want a sale to go through, or a deal to be agreed on.

We want a strategic goal to be accepted by the team so we can all get to work on making it happen. Use your body language early and often to put people in the mood to agree with you.

Studies show that by starting a conversation in an open, engaging way, you can set the other participants up to agree with you.

Remember that mirroring concept? Where other people will mirror the body language they like, or mirror the person they want to be like? We are designed to want to adopt the posture of what is pleasant to us, so start by being that example! Walk into a room smiling, with an upright and welcoming posture.

Practice comfortable, cheerful eye contact and give your colleagues the positive signals of engagement. They will want to mirror your openness! As they begin to adopt your attitude, and your posture, you'll see that they become more open as well. This is the perfect time to pitch your idea for the business, ask for that raise, or pick the destination for lunch!

Your physical workspace can affect how open you are perceived to be. If our body language communicates openness, then the way we are set up at work can change the way our bodies communicate this message. Think about your office, or the common meeting room. Are certain chairs higher or better than others? How do people sit when talking? Are they directly opposite each other? Is the table between them?

Consider that we actually look for other people's body language as a comforting way to better understand what they are saying. If we are robbed of these additional visual cues, it can be harder for us to understand one another through body language. A restrictive work space can rob us of these important touch points of body language. That's why open workspaces feel so much more accommodating and social.

We are being presented with the many important visual cues that allow us to connect better with each other, and truly collaborate. So maybe it's time to carve out an open conversation area in your office, to allow people's body language to be interpreted correctly and fully.

Put others at Ease

It usually pays to put other people at ease. Whether it's your boyfriend or girlfriend, an unhappy customer at work, or even your boss, the less tension a conversation carries the better! So it's important to be able to recognize other people's tension or anxiousness, and attempt to diffuse it with your own body language.

Do you see those arms being crossed, or feet pointing toward the door? These are the giveaway signs that someone is feeling discomfort, and wanting to leave. You can help change their mind simply by adjusting their body language! Just like with smiling and frowning, changing body language can induce mental changes!

Engage the person with their arms crossed by handing them something, like a ball or a piece of paper. Just getting them to uncross those arms and engage you a little bit will help put them in less of a defensive posture.

When to "Square Up"

In general, squaring up shows the other person you are engaged and interested. It's a signal that you are being respectful, and attentive. But knowing when and how to use the square up has further nuance.

Just as too much eye contact can be intimidating, too much squaring up can become confrontational. This is particularly true for men, because confrontation is typically more common among male groups. You will notice that when two men are talking, they rarely face each other directly. Usually both men will assume an angle that is slightly away from the other. This is actually more comfortable for men, because in cases of confrontation men will face each other directly in order to assert dominance. So in casual conversation, it becomes more accessible for men to take these slightly contorted angles.

Women are more likely to view the squaring up as a positive component of body language. When deciding how to square up to someone you're talking to, take gender into account!

Don't square up too much to a man unless you want to convey intimacy, or possibly conflict! Use the square up with women to convey respect without risking conflict.

Relax!

Over the previous chapters you've learned a lot about the body language of tension. Tension appears in all of our negative emotions, and it is evident all over the body. Tension is one of those elements that will grip you and control your body language, corrupt your vocal variety, and distort your message. Even if you're just an extrovert, sometimes your outgoing energy can create tension with other people. Do you work with a technical team of introverts?

Are you an extrovert? Recognize that your energy and enthusiasm can be stressful for them. Watch their body language curl up to protect themselves from you, but don't be offended. Match their energy by relaxing a little. This will put them more at ease, and allow you to converse more freely with them.

Respect Others

One of the best lessons for monitoring someone's body language is to respect them with your own. The goal of body language isn't simple domination! If that were the case, you'd have rooms of corporate executives standing on chairs with open arms, screaming their conversations across the room.

The key to succeeding with your understanding of body language is to use it to make other people more comfortable.

You should tune your senses to better intuit the mood in a room, the emotions of another person, the goals or aspirations they have, so that you can help! If someone is uncomfortable, recognize that and do your best to make them comfortable. If someone is angry or agitated, realize whether or not you're the cause and do your best to address the conflict before it gets out of control! Match your energy to other people's energy, so as not to make them defensive or anxious.

Manage other people's expectations of you by knowing whether or not they are actually attracted to you, or if they want to leave the room as soon as possible. The best thing you can do with your new understanding people's body language is help them!

In this chapter you have learnt how to comport yourself so as to be more successful around other people, whether it is in your workplace or your home life. Remember that the body language of other people is a rich tapestry of signals, and that no single signal tells the entire story. Those crossed arms could simply mean the room is colder than usual! They might not mean your significant other isn't receptive to your idea for a new TV! Read the entire cluster of signals, and make your determination based on all the information you're getting.

Final Words

Here's a final thought exercise for you. Think about all the text message conversations we have in our world today! What percentage of the overall communication picture are you really getting with a text message? Research tells us that simple verbal communication (the words themselves) accounts for less than 10% of the intended message.

Our physical body language is capable of delivering over half of the total message content, and the simple nuanced ways we deliver our words is responsible for the rest!

It's interesting then to consider emojis, small graphical depictions of body language (a genuine smile, a fake smile, sweat, anxiousness) as natural additions to the text message and instant message world, because they represent crucial clues we use to interact more completely with each other.

You've seen that much of our communication comes from nonverbal cues, and that many of these cues are gifted to us from our evolution. We cover and protect ourselves when we are nervous or scared, by closing our bodies off and covering our necks.

When we are confident or ambitious, we raise our profiles to be above others in the room, we raise our volume and our speech patterns to suit our goals.

Remember that no one cue tells the whole story. Most people are aware of their body language at some level, and will try to manipulate it to suit their goals. But few people are capable of manipulating all of these cues at once (do you think you could control the size of your pupils the next time you're talking to your boss?). That's why it's important to view a conversation with someone as a conversation with their whole person, all of their cues simultaneously. Let one cue pique your interest, and follow that up with more observation of the other available cues.

Is that awkward eye contact starting to make you wonder if the person is lying to you? Now check the other signs. Are they closing off from you, or backing away somehow? Are they otherwise uncomfortable and appearing ready to head for the door? When they do break eye contact, where do their eyes go? Are they headed off to the right, to conjure another detail for the lie, or to the left to remember exactly what happened?

This is how you build a picture of someone's emotional state through consistent interpretation and analysis of the available cues. Let your instinct guide you to a theory, and use your new understanding of science to do deeper research!

Use this information to further your career by deepening your relationships with colleagues. Give them the emotional support they need by better understanding what they need in the workplace from you. Use this information to serve your personal relationships. Become more respectful of your family, friends and significant others. By mastering these small tips, you can become more insightful and intuitive in their eyes. You'll "just seem to know" when they need things, or when they're thinking about something else.

Finally, learning body language is about understanding what you need! Sometimes you think you're the sole master and proprietor of what's happening in your head, but start observing your own body language and you might learn something. The next time you're in a meeting and you cross your arms and legs, or notice where you've pointed your feet, you might just learn that you're unhappier than you thought with a particular statement or direction.

You might realize that you have some secrets hidden just beyond your conscious mind, ready to be learned and used to your advantage! By adjusting your body language, you can start to adjust your own thoughts and your own mood.

Assume a more confident body position, and you'll find you feel more confident. It's how our bodies work! Stand up straight, smile more, and try to remain as open as you can.

You'll find you have more followers, more fans, and stronger relationships with people who admire you and want to be around you!

Thank you for reading this book. It has been a pleasure to write it. Can I ask you a favor? If you can spare a few minutes, could you please leave a review about this book? It helps me to produce even more books about this topic.

Good luck analyzing people!

www.ingramcontent.com/pod-product-compliance
Lightning Source LLC
Chambersburg PA
CBHW061232180526
45170CB00003B/1267